HOW SUCCESS
BECAME MY FOCUS

Jameel Davis

PAGE PUBLISHING, INC.
New York, NY

First originally published by Page Publishing, Inc. 2015

ISBN 978-1-63417-200-4 (pbk)
ISBN 978-1-63417-201-1 (digital)

Printed in the United States of America

Acknowledgements

First and foremost, I would to thank the Creator for showing me my purpose in life and for allowing it to impact others in a positive way. I give thanks to the creator for providing me with a beautiful family, for placing me in a safe living environment, for allowing me to have my finances in order and for making my success possible.

I would like to thank my mother Louise Davis for raising me into an incredible man. I also would like to thank her for being one of my greatest support systems. Without her and her teachings of life's lessons, I would not have accomplished what I've accomplished this far in life.

I would like to thank my grandparents and other family members for believing in me when everyone else was in doubt. Their comfort and encouraging words and support give me confidence and strength to achieve whatever I put my mind to. A special recognition to my grandfathers Alan Williamson and Gerard Davis for showing me where I came from, because that allowed me to see where I'm headed.

I would like to personally thank my partner and better half Bobbiestarr Horton for her role in my achievements this year. My recent and rapid growth is in result of her consistent love, encouragement and support. A special thanks to this beautiful woman for assisting in typing "How Success Became My Focus."

I truly appreciate Page Publishing, Bruce Baker, and my Publication Coordinator Casey Runyan for making "How Success Became My Focus" possible. I never thought I would become a published author and they made this huge achievement possible.

Last and not least: I would like to express my gratitude to the many people who saw me through this book; to all those who have been with me over the course of the years and those who I've recently connected with.

Have you ever felt so lost in life that you don't know where you are heading to? Do you ever feel like giving up even after you've given your all? Does it seem like your best isn't just enough? Well, worry no more. Set aside your anxieties, be inspired, and reach greater heights with *How Success Became My Focus*

With enthusiasm, Jameel Davis will stir your passion and divert your energies toward determination as he shares his success story. He overcame his struggles and emerged from being an ordinary student to a successful and respectable individual that he is now. Geared toward success, Davis was able to motivate himself to stand out from others and better himself. He steered his life around and directed his momentum to the path that aided him to rise from his downfall. Despite life's pitfalls, Davis was able to conquer it all through his willpower. So if ever you feel down and discouraged, never lose hope. Always remember that there is more to life. Come out from your shell like Davis did and be an inspiration to others. Go out, inspire, and stand out with *How Success Became My Focus*

On August 21, 1989, I was born to Louise Davis and John Chavers. My mother was thirteen years old at the time of my birth, and she was still a virgin. My father was seventeen years old at the time and nowhere to be found. My mother got pregnant when my father's preejaculation made contact with my mother's vagina without penetration. My grandmother suggested my mother to get an abortion, but after further communication, my mother was able to keep and deliver me. My grandmother told me since the first day my mother delivered me. She took great care of me. "She was a great mother at thirteen years old." My mother began teaching my grandmother parenting skills. At such a young age, my mother helped care for her brother, her sister, and me.

Without a father figure around, my mother knew she couldn't just sit back and wait for help, so she took action. She worked, received government assistance—food stamps, medical, dental, vision, child care, and a lot more. My mother told me that she used to bathe me three times a day as a baby. I began walking at eight months old and began riding a bike without training wheels at three years old. I attended the same day care as my aunt and uncle. My aunt was two years old going on three and my uncle was five years old and I was three years old.

January 5, 1993, my mother gave birth to my little sister Tahja Mosley. My mother was seventeen years old at the time. My sister's father was not around at the time and still isn't present day. With neither of our fathers around, my mother did not give up. She took care of her business and made sure my sister and I had adequate food, water, light, ventilation, temperate, control sanitation, medical care, clothing, and bedding, access to toilet, lavatory and showers.

A year later, after my sister was born, my mother moved out of my grandmother's house and into the Cleveland Metropolitan Housing Authority (CMHA) apartments located on Central Avenue in Cleveland, Ohio. The Cuyahoga Metropolitan Housing Authority (CMHA) owns and manages property and administers rent subsidy programs to provide eligible low-income persons good, affordable housing. The community we lived in was a high poverty and high crime community. I attended the local elementary school up the street, Marion Sterling. I had to repeat the first grade due to attendance. My second chance at first grade was an embarrassment; kids at school laughed and picked on me about it. However, my attendance was better, and I made excellent grades every year since.

Summer of 1998, I was playing T-ball for the local recreation center, "central recreation center." After returning home from my first game, I was notified of some disturbing news regarding my mother and another woman who lived in the same neighborhood. My mother and the other woman had gotten into a verbal dispute and later in a physical altercation that ended with my mother serving two years in the state penitentiary for felonious assault. On the day of her sentencing, I was at school. When I got home from school at around 2:45 p.m., my grandmother was there, and my mother wasn't. I then asked my grandmother where my mom was, and she told me, "They kept her…they gave her two years." I immediately started crying, and my grandmother joined me. I was hurt bad. With my mother gone away to prison and no father around, my sister and I were forced to live with my grandparents over the next two years. I changed schools and homes three times due to my grandparent's financial difficulties. Although they did a great job at taking care of my sister and me, as well as their kids over the period my mother was away from us.

Out of the three schools, two that I attended were difficult to adjust too: Moses Cleveland Elementary School and Adlai Stevenson Elementary School. Academically they weren't, but getting the respect from other students was hard. I was always defending myself from problem children. Fighting wasn't a hobby of mine, but I had to in order to keep the bullies away. Moving multiple times had a major impact on me because it ruined friendships. I had to start over every time we moved. Also there were neighborhood bullies every time we moved that I had to fight off. No matter the obstacles, I faced while changing schools and moving multiple times while my mother was away, I still did well in school. I did well because I knew my grandparents would reward me. My aunt, uncle, and sister didn't do as well as I did in school and at home; so they weren't rewarded as much. That treatment caused problems at home, such as arguments and fights between them and me. They hated to see me get rewarded. But it didn't make them work harder in school or behave properly.

December 31, 2000, my mom returned home from prison. My grandmother surprised everyone by bringing my mother home while everyone was asleep, so when we woke up, we can be in total shock. Her arrival was a Christmas wish and a New Year's celebration. I had my mother back. Since then, my mother has not done anything to jeopardize losing her children again, and she has developed into a loving and responsible mother. Without her valuable teachings of life's lessons, I would not have accomplished what I've accomplished this far in life. I have learned my parenting and survival skills from her. She has been there when I hit every obstacle, and she has helped me fight through them. She has witnessed my biggest accomplishments in life, and her presence meant more to me than me receiving the actual rewards.

After the third time we moved, I attended Union Elementary School as a fifth grader and lived in the Union neighborhood. Union elementary was a great school. Many of the children were well behaved, and teachers were able to get through their lesson plans. My first time getting suspended from school was at Union elementary, and I cried. I had gotten into a fight with another student (self-defense), and the principal Mrs. Washington gave me three to five days suspension. I hated to miss school, ever since I got held back in the first grade. After my suspension was over, I returned to school and did superior in my academics. At graduation, I graduated in the top ten of my class and received many awards and certificates.

As a young African American male growing up in the inner city of Cleveland, Ohio, I did not have a strong support system or many resources that inspired me to develop a positive lifestyle. The residential communities, in which I have resided, were primarily resource free. The communities were and still are densely populated urban communities that are plagued by high violence and high poverty. Low quality schools are located in the minority dominated communities in which I have resided. The local schools are minority dominated and over-crowded, which means more violence. The only resources I remember growing up were local churches and recreation centers that offered free lunch to the local youth. I was one of the youth that took full advantage of the free meals that was offered by the churches and recreation centers. I did not take advantage of the meals because I was a starving child, but because it was free to the youth. I do not recall a time when my sister and I were hungry and could not eat. Due to the welfare food stamps our mother received from the government, she was able to keep food in the home.

I did not have a role model growing up. There was no one that I looked up to.

The only positive insight I received growing up came from family and others. They would tell me to stay in school and get good grades. I did as was told. During elementary school, I never understood the importance of education. All I knew was get good grades. I did not know what that would lead me to. Outside of school, I hung out with peers that was not doing well in school and that had behavior problems. They would bully other kids, steal, use profanity, etc. There were not many positive kids in my neighborhood. Many of the children's parents were not supportive or communicative. Their home environments exposed the children to aggression, abuse, and violence, which the children picked up and used toward others. My mother and grandparents were very supportive and communicative with me when I was a child and an adolescent. They told me what to do and what not to do, and I listened. I was praised and treated for great work and behavior. I knew that if I did poorly in school, I would not receive special rewards and treatment.

It was not until I was thirteen years old when I finally understood the importance of education. Thirteen years of age, living in densely populated urban communities that are plagued by high violence and high poverty, I was faced with drug dealers, drug abusers, homeless individuals, victims of domestic violence, rapists, victims of sexual assault, and many other victims of crime and criminals. I have witnessed many individuals commit various crimes, and I have witnessed many victims of crime. Watching neighborhoods get destroyed and watching individuals throw their life away made me understand the importance of education. I knew I did not want to live my life the way the people in my community were living theirs, and education was the way out of violent and poverty dominated neighborhoods. I did not want to become a product of my community.

I remember times as a teen when I would go to the local store or supermarket, and adults would be standing outside asking everyone that walked by for change. I was mind blown by the experiences because it is traditional for kids and teens to ask adults for money to go to the store, not for adults to be asking the youth outside of the store. After experiencing the negative events in my neighborhood, I told myself that "I will never do anything to put me behind bars and that I will not be the adult standing outside the store asking for money."

I attended Albert B. Hart Middle School from 2001 to 2004. I was involved in basketball, soccer, and an accelerated reading program. I maintained excellent grades. I was determined to succeed. Nothing could stop my success. During the sixth and seventh grade, I ignored all the negative people around me and focused on basketball and my studies. As a player on the boys basketball and soccer team, players grades determined whether we played or not. I loved the game of basketball, my family and peers enjoyed watching me play for my school. I made sure my grades were excellent, and I was on my best behavior each week so that I could play in the scheduled games. Homework and sports practice kept me out of trouble. My schoolwork was completed before I did anything else. I would get home from school and do my homework before eating dinner. After my schoolwork was completed, I would even hang out with the problematic youth in my community. Education was my number one goal.

During the 2003 to 2004 school year, I recall sitting in my eighth-grade English class when I was called down to the school's library to meet with a gentleman by the name of Joe Klir. Joe Klir was at Albert B. Hart Middle School, recruiting a few eighth grade students for the Rotsky Foundation for Mentors program. The Rotsky Foundation for Mentors was created to provide hope, motivation, and encouragement to Cleveland Public School students. The foundation partners inner-city middle school students (protégés) with local professionals (mentors) that work in a field of interest to the student. I spoke with Mr. Klir regarding the program and what it had to offer. After my meeting with Mr. Klir, I decided to join the Rotsky Foundation for Mentors. It was time for me to have a positive role model that would guide me on the right path to success.

Leon Anderson III became my mentor in the Rotsky Foundation for Mentors program. Leon Anderson III is the president of Sports and Spine Physical Therapy Inc. Mr. Anderson became my role model. His lectures and speeches inspired and motivated me to succeed. Not only was he my role model, he was also my teacher. Mr. Anderson taught me the importance of responsibilities and the importance of goals. He once told me to write down all my goals and to write down the names of everyone that has ever doubted me. He told me to keep them next to my bed on my nightstand. Although I never wrote down the names of the people that doubted me, I did write down my goals. Mr. Anderson stayed on me about my schoolwork. I could not wear a hat or wave cap on my head around him unless I had straight A's on my report cards.

Early April 2004, I was invited by the Rotsky Foundation for Mentors to attend the Day in the Life program at Case Western Reserve University. Every year, the Rotsky Foundation for Mentors invites all protégés to Case Western Reserve University to experience the Day in the Life of a College Student. During the event, mentors and protégés come together to enjoy food, games, and to speak about their college experience. The day would end with motivational speakers and a scholarship ceremony for the high school graduating seniors. Attending Case Western Reserve University to shadow a student was my first taste of what it was like to be a college student. I have always thought college was boring and very hard. Case Western Reserve University changed my views on college. Case Western Reserve made college interesting for me, and I was desperate to attend college after the Day in the Life program. I was only in the eighth grade. I knew in order for me to make it to college. I had to stay focused on my education and maintain excellent grades. With Mr. Anderson as my mentor and teacher and with the help of the Rotsky Foundation for mentors, I was going to make that happen.

June 2004, it was the day of my eighth-grade awards and graduation ceremony. Upon my entrance into the school auditorium, I was greeted with a long blue ribbon that was worn across my upper body. After receiving my ribbon, I was seated in the first row on the stage. At that time, I did not know what the ribbon stood for and why I was in the front row. Prior to the day of graduation, I did know that I would be introducing our keynote speaker. Principal Rudolph selected Judge Deane Buchanan of Cleveland Heights Municipal Court as the keynote speaker for the eighth-grade graduation ceremony. As nervous as I was to be on the stage in front of hundreds of people, I was honored to have read Judge Deane Buchanan's biography, and I was honored to have introduced him to the audience and graduates. The awards ceremony began at the conclusion of his speech, and he remained at the ceremony until the conclusion. My name was called for almost every award that was being presented. Almost every time I sat down in my seat I was getting right back up to receive another. The audience, my family, and Judge Deane Buchanan were highly impressed. I received awards, such as honor role, perfect attendance, citizenship, and many more. I had no idea that I would be receiving multiple awards and certificates.

Soon after the awards ceremony, the graduation ceremony began. The first ten seats on the stage were for the students that were at the top ten percent of the class. One of those seats was assigned to me. All top ten graduates wore a ribbon around their upper body. I believed I graduated third in my class. At the conclusion of the ceremony, I was greeted by Judge Deane Buchanan whom was excited of my accomplishments. He was so proud of my accomplishments that he told me to contact him upon graduating from college. I added that task to my list of goals.

I spent the summer of 2004 hanging with friends and practicing my basketball skills. High school was approaching, and I had the choice of attending South High School (public school) or Lutheran High School East (private school). Both high school head basketball coaches wanted me to play on their team. I decided to attend South High School because I wanted to show people that it is possible to succeed in the Cleveland Municipal School District.

August 2004 was the start of the 2004–2005 school year. I was nervous on the first day of high school like any other freshman would have been. South High School was an overcrowded, low quality, minority dominated school located in a high poverty, high-crime community. There was a lot of gang activity and violence going on in the school. South High had a high dropout rate. Females became young mothers, which forced them to miss school and eventually drop out. Males were involved in gang activity that either got them expelled, arrested, or killed. Students with low self-esteem were made fun of and bullied, which caused them to miss school and eventually dropout. Students that were exposed to aggression, abuse, and violence at their home began to reduce their attendance and stopped going to school. Many students dropped out of school when they could not pass all five parts of the Ohio Graduation Test before graduating from High School. The OGT consisted of writing, reading, math, science, and social studies. Students became extremely frustrated after repeated poor test scores. That frustration allowed them to lose focus of their future and dropout. Many did not take advantage of the tutoring that was provided to help students pass the OGT.

With all the negative energy going on around me in the school, I was still able to remain focused on my studies. I had a few altercations and arguments in and out of school. Many of those incidents arouse because others tried to take advantage of me by attempting to bully me. My self-defense tactics that was obtained from local street fighters and boxing centers kept them away. I was always taught to defend myself. I knew that the negative energy and people around me was God's test for me. He wanted to see if I can avoid obstacles and if not avoid them; fight through them to get to my goals.

Soon I became involved in soccer, cross-country and basketball. I received trophies in soccer and in cross-country for my outstanding talent. I was not able to play basketball my first season because I tore my ACL in my left knee during basketball practice the week before our first game. I was crushed; I knew I would never play the game like I once did before. My basketball dream of playing in the NBA was gone. The NBA wanted good, healthy players. Professional basketball was not God's plan for me; he had something else in store for me.

I did my rehabilitation therapy with Sports and Spine Physical Therapy, my mentor Leon Anderson's company at no charge. How great was that? I sustained an injury, and my mentor was there to treat my injury and to help me get ready for the upcoming basketball season. The following school year had rolled around, and I was now a sophomore in high school.

I became a member of the Sports Management program. The program was offered to sophomores with a grade point average of a 3.0 and above. The program ran from tenth grade to graduation and focused on the structure of the human body. South High School was one of two schools in the United States that offered the program to high school students. Once accepted the students, were required to maintain a 2.5 or 3.0 grade point average in order to remain in the program.

I excelled in sports management as sophomore. I was among the few students that were at the top of the class. My good friend Shaunnora Buchalter (graduate of Case Western Reserve University), my friend since Albert B. Hart Middle School, whom also was a part of the Rotsky Foundation for Mentors programs joined me in the Sports Management Program at South High. We were one another's motivation to do well in school. We would inspire each other to give our all in our studies. We and other student's that were at the top of our sports management class like my good friend Ronald Blair (graduate of Mount Union College) would challenge each other academically. We would see who can get the most points on projects, homework, reports, exams, and all other assignments. Our teacher would post the grades on the board each week, and we would all compete for being number one or at least in the top five. We would compete every week. We pushed each other to succeed. Outside of sports management, I also excelled in all of my other courses. My goal was to graduate high school in the top 10 percent of my class.

By junior year, I was highly recognized for my outstanding accomplishments. I was amongst one of the smartest juniors in the Cleveland Municipal School District and surrounding school districts. My chemistry teacher, Michael Robinson, nominated me to be one of the outstanding juniors in math and science for the Cleveland

Technical Societies Council. Soon, I was notified by the Cleveland Technical Societies Council that I was amongst one of four juniors in the Cleveland Municipal School District, invited to attend the scholarship and achievement awards and banquet ceremony. The scholarship and achievement awards ceremony was held at Landerhaven by Executive Caterers in Mayfield Heights, Ohio for students in North East Ohio. The other three students that had accompanied me were Shakayla Rainey (Cleveland East High), Marissa Allen (Cleveland School of the Arts), and Sarah Decorlo (John Marshall High School). "Notice they all were females." Our teachers that nominated us accompanied us at the ceremony/banquet.

I joined Youth Opportunities Unlimited (YOU) at the end of my junior year. The program was a youth empowerment program at the Friendly Inn Settlement Center. Its mission was to empower high school youth to succeed in school, in the workplace and in life through education, employment, and entrepreneurship. YOU created programs that motivated youth to stay in school and graduate by adding a comprehensive and intensive career coaching component to their employability skills curriculum. In the summer of 2007, the Friendly Inn Settlement Center offered an all-expense paid college tour for the students involved in the program. We visited thirteen different colleges and universities located in North Carolina, South Carolina and Virginia.

I was determined to finish high school strong. Senior year was here and I was an honor roll member. I received the Business Tech Student of the month award, and I was recognized on the occasion of the Rotary Club of Cleveland's Thirtieth Annual Thesmacher High School recognition Day for my outstanding achievements. I met all the requirements for graduation and was set to go. However, I had a major dilemma; I hadn't applied to any colleges or filled out for FASFA.

The Rotsky Foundation had awarded me a one-thousand-dollar freshman scholarship to use for my educational needs at the annual Day in the Life program at the Case Western Reserve University.

Prom was approaching, and I was excited to go. I was so focused on prom and senior activities that I didn't think about college. Our senior activities and prom was a great outcome and a memorable experience.

On the day of the Senior Awards Ceremony, I received many awards and certificates much as I did at my middle school graduation ceremony and elementary school graduation. I wasn't shocked that I received them because I knew I had earned them. But there was one award that I was really surprised I received and that was "Excellence in Writing." At the time of the announcement, I was goofing around with my classmates in the audience. Mr. Wilson and Mrs. Johnson both English teachers were presenting the certificate and gift out. "Jameel Davis," they called, I was totally shocked. I knew they were going to call someone else for the award. I went and accepted the award. I never enjoyed writing; in fact, I hated writing. Although I got positive feedback on all of my writing assignments, I didn't believe my writing was that good. "It was my weakness, in my opinion." I thanked Mr. Wilson and Mrs. Johnson for seeing the potential in my writing when I couldn't.

On graduation day; I was seated in the front row amongst other individuals. We were the top ten graduates of our graduating class. I graduated third in my high school class. My friends Juanita Clipper was valedictorian and Shaunnora Buchalter was salutatorian. Although, I wasn't number one in my graduation class, I was the only graduate with an honors diploma. "I had graduated with honors." To me, that was better than being valedictorian. My diploma is different than all the others. I have a special gold pendant on it titled "Diploma with Honors."

I spent the summer of 2008 celebrating my high school graduation, reading through shoe boxes full of college letters, filling out FASFA and applying to colleges. August had arrived and I hadn't made a decision to which college I wanted to attend. It was so many schools to choose from and narrowing down schools to choose from was very difficult do to transportation and financial reasons. My family and I didn't have the money to travel to the open houses that the colleges or universities had wanted me to attend. I wasn't working at that time, so I didn't have money to put gas in my car to make the road trips.

Many schools were very expensive, and my financial aid didn't cover it. My academics didn't qualify me for full scholarships. I was forced to apply to cheaper schools that my financial aid would cover. My aid consisted of grants/loans.

During the first two weeks of August, I was calling schools non-stop trying to get accepted with the aid money I had. "I had no luck." It was almost the start of the third week of August, and I was not accepted into any college. "I was frustrated." However, I kept trying and trying. Finally I received a call one morning from Salem International University in Salem, West Virginia, telling me they wanted me to attend their school. They told me to fill out an application and to add them to my FAFSA application. At the end of the call, I did what I was told and Map Quested the distance from my home (three hours and forty-five minutes) "not bad at all." The next morning, I received a call from Salem International University saying I was accepted into their school and that I was invited down to attend student orientation. I was also contacted by the basketball coach the next day. I used the money from the part-time temporary job I had got in the beginning of August to pay for the trip to Salem, WV. My mother and girlfriend at the time accompanied me on the trip.

We arrived in a small town called Salem located in West Virginia the next day. Upon our arrival, we were directed to the academic center were orientation was held. With Salem International University having a very small campus, the academic center was easy to locate. I don't remember any details about the orientation. I remember walking around the campus with my mother and girlfriend, and I was very excited about attending college. I didn't care about the campus size, the people there at the time of orientation or anything; I was ready to start classes.

At the end of orientation, we headed back to Cleveland, Ohio, and I brought back school shirts for my family. Upon our arrival, we shared the news about the school to family and friends and arranged a going-away to college party for the upcoming Saturday. Friends and family helped me celebrate this special event. My mother prepared a delicious meal for everyone to enjoy. The evening was filled with fun, laughs, music, and good supportive individuals. Knowing that I would be leaving for college the following day, my Mother and Grandma were very emotional. "They cried happy tears" and gave the longest and most touching hugs I've ever had. I began to cry with them. They were proud of me but they didn't want me to be that far away from home. I had to do what was best for me: get an education so I can have a brighter future.

Classes had begun. I was excited and determined to do well. I had my class schedule, and it was time to start the journey to success. When I first saw my schedule, I was excited about attending every class except for college English. I was nervous about taking college English because, as I mentioned before, I wasn't confident in my writing ability. I believed my writing wasn't good at all. My English professor Mrs. Lynn Wise helped me change my thoughts about my writing ability. She made writing exciting to me. She showed me how to write proper essays, although she thought my writing was excellent. She told me the only thing I was missing in my essays and writing assignments were transition words. Once she introduced me to transition words and different styles of writing, I took my writing to a whole new level. I became more confident and I was writing A+ essay and research papers. Mrs. Lynn Wise made me love writing, she's the reason I'm writing today.

College English made all of my other classes a lot easier since most had to do with power point, research papers, and projects. I had all the tools I needed to excel in English class. One thing English didn't prepare me for was public speaking, a weakness I had at the time. Not that I was afraid of people, but I was more afraid of having the wrong choice of words or stuttering. The student success and orientation course for freshmen have helped me overcome my fear of public speaking. We had about fifty-plus freshmen in the class, and most of our assignments were focused on class interactions and group assignments. It was one class assignment the professor assigned that had me really nervous. The assignment was to create a power point presentation about Salem International University and how the school plans to help me achieve my goals. The presentation had to be presented in front of the entire class and was graded based on the information presented, the structure of the power point, eye contact, citation, loudness, knowledge of the topic, plagiarism, and audience interaction.

I froze when I read the rubric for the presentation. I didn't know what to write about. I turned to the academic support center (student support services) for help. There, I had tutors and professional staff members helping me with my assignment. They helped me picked out my topic, write about it, organize it, and present it. I was in the student support services center every day until presentation day working and practicing my presentation. I practiced eye contact, voice, structure of slides, and information. All the skills I needed to get an A on the project.

The day came for us to present and the professor asked, "Who would like to go first?" I raised my hand quickly and said, "I will go." I worked hard on my presentation. I had a lot of practice. I was ready to go. I dimmed the lights in the lecture hall because my presentation was about the history of SIU and how it will help contribute to my road to success. I wanted my audience to feel comfortable and relaxed while at the same time wide awake. The way I delivered my presentation, I did just that. I was energetic, moving around the room. My eyes was on the audience more than the slides. I had a great tone of voice, I use enthusiasm in my words, I interacted with my audience, the right choice of words was rolling off my tongue; and I was feeling good inside. At the conclusion of my presentation, I had a big round of applause from my audience and received great responses from everyone in the class (which I still have today). My professor pulled me to the side after the last presentation that was held that day and told me, "Outstanding job, Jameel…Thank you." I gave a special thanks to Student Support Services for helping me do an outstanding job on my presentation and for helping me succeed in all my other courses.

The first semester had come to an end. I had a GPA of 4.0. I finished my first semester of college with all "As." I was then placed on the dean's list and received an academic achievement award from student support services for maintaining a 3.0 or higher for the first semester. I was very proud of myself.

I began the second semester with the same attitude, excited and determined to do well. I started off the semester with a great start, getting A's on all my assignments, quizzes, and exams. I was feeling like a scholar.

On February 16, 2009, my application to attend the Ann Crum Banquet (WVAEOPP eighth annual student leadership conference) at Davis and Elkins College in Elkins, West Virginia was approved. I was selected on behalf of Salem International University and Student Support Services to represent SSS at the leadership conference. The conference was held to recognize outstanding students and their achievements from various colleges or universities in Northern West Virginia. I did it in Ohio, and I did it again in West Virginia. I was on the road to success.

The rest of the second semester was smooth sailing. I finished my freshman year of college with a GPA of 4.0 ("As" in every course). I didn't have the full college experience that I was hoping for at Salem. There was little to do on the small campus, with lack of activities and fun. I chose to focus more of my time on my education. Although I did enjoy playing basketball, ping pong, Nintendo Wii, etc., with my peers from all different backgrounds.

Packing up and leaving Salem, I knew I didn't want to return in the fall. I was grateful for all that I've learned at Salem, but I was ready for the full college experience: campus activities, parties, girls, sports etc. Also I was ready to move closer to my family and friends (I had missed them).

During summer break, I went ahead and applied to Cleveland State University, the University of Akron, Ursline College, John Carroll University, Tiffin University and Kent State University. I narrowed my choices to three school: Cleveland State University, the University of Akron, and Kent State University. By the end of the summer, I chose to attend Kent State University for the 2009 to 2010 school year to continue my studies in Criminal Justice. I didn't select Cleveland State University because it was too close to home, and I believe I wouldn't be as focused like I needed to be. I would have been distracted by family members, violence, and peer pressure. The University of Akron was located near a high-crime area, and I wouldn't have been comfortable there either. I needed some where not too far from home but in a community where I would feel safe. Kent State University was that place.

I was amazed by Kent's beautifully large campus. The landscape made the campus seem peaceful and welcoming. Since the first day on campus, I knew I would be a graduate of Kent State University. I've witnessed student organizations participating on and off campus that made me become a proud student of Kent State University. Knowing Kent State was a party school, I couldn't wait to party and to meet new people from various walks of life. After attending my first Kent State party, I was desperate to have more fun. But I knew in order to keep the fun going, I had to stay on top of my studies and maintain good grades.

My goal was to complete as many class assignments as I could before the weekend approached. I was determined to kick it on the weekends with my college friends. I began reading over my syllabi and completed all the major assignments first. Monday to Wednesday were the days I was most productive with my schoolwork. I was knocking out papers, projects, studying, study guides, etc., way before the due date. I made sure my major course work was completed by Wednesday night or Thursday morning so I could enjoy the upcoming weekend (Thursday night to Saturday night). That was my system. I would party so much and have so much fun. People thought I wasn't in school. "Work first, party later."

I met so many people fall semester and eventually became popular on campus. Other students enjoyed my positive energy, leadership, confidence, intelligence, and sense of humor. They really enjoyed the fact that I was very outgoing. My characteristics helped me build strong friendships and a strong support system. Others loved my company; they would turn to me for advice and guidance.

The wonderful people I met and Kent State's academic support center (SSS) helped motivate me to do well in my classes. If I slacked, I could be put on academic probation and/or suspended for a semester. I finished fall semester '09 by being placed on the College of Arts and Sciences dean's list for my superior academic achievement. I went ahead and finished the spring semester the same way.

Using my same system to maintain my grades, junior year of college was a breeze as far as course work went. At one point of time during my junior year, I became in deep thought with myself, I wasn't sure of myself and what my purpose was on this earth. I asked myself one day,

"Who am I?" I was clueless. I knew that I was intelligent, hardworking, funny, confident, loving; but I didn't know me deep down inside. I didn't know my role in life; all I knew was go to school and get good grades. I felt incomplete, I was lost with myself.

One day I sat down and I began to write…I wrote down a list of questions to ask myself, and I had answered them with a great response. After writing down my answers, I read them and then turned the questions and answers into "Jameel's Motivational Creed," a piece I could recite and memorize if I ever got into deep thought again.

> Who are you? I am a man! What kind of man? A self-motivated black man! What is your purpose? My purpose is to be a leader and be the change in society by striving for success and helping as many people as I can along the way! What do you have to offer? I offer a mind filled with the intelligence I need to make it to the top, I offer a heart filled with love that is ready to explode, I offer strength and effort that allows me to take on any challenge and I don't give up easily! Why don't you give up easily? One who gives up easy is considered lazy and weak; therefore, I work hard at every task! Why do you work hard? Working hard allows me to turn hard obstacles into easy ones and hard work builds my character and builds my self-confidence! Who do you look up to? I look up to myself; why do you look up to yourself? Because I am superior than many, at the same level as most and not too far from the ones at the top! So who are you??? I'm Jameel; who is Jameel? A man of his word, a leader filled with pride, courage, love, intelligence, humor, respect, confidence and most of all, a black man with a plan! What's your plan? My plan is to act as a magnet and attract all I need in order to succeed and be a change for myself and society.

Upon turning my questions and answers into a creed and reading it a few times, I felt happy inside. Those words I wrote in response to my questions were who I was. I read it over and over numerous times so I could memorize and recite it. I even made a slide show with pictures of me, with music playing in the background with the words showing on the screen. I voice recorded me reading it so I could play it back to back. Within a couple days, I had it memorized. I still know it until this day.

My motivational creed had become the force in pushing me to be a successful, responsible individual. It was the key factor in helping me finish my junior year in great academic standings, and it will be the key factor in my future accomplishments. The 2011–2012 school year had approached, and I was a "Super Senior," meaning it will be a least two semesters before I graduate due to unfinished credit requirements. While working part-time in college, I had to limit the amount of courses I could take each semester. College of Arts and Sciences program had an intense credit requirement that needed to be obtained before graduation. So my graduation date was moved to May 11, 2013. I wasn't upset about it. I just continued to work hard and stay motivated.

I spent the 2011 to 2012 school year meeting the credit requirements. I enrolled in more classes and slowed down on the partying. I didn't want my graduation to be pushed back even further.

May 25, 2012, Alayna Teague gave birth to our son Jaheir Davonne Davis.

Alayna and I had only been dating for a few months before she became pregnant. After she found out she was pregnant, she suggested abortion and adoption, and I suggested she keep it even though I didn't have the finances to take care of an infant at the time. I knew I would be a great father and that I would find a way to take care of him. After communicating, we agreed she keep him. Jaheir D. Davis was born four weeks earlier (premature) 3 lbs. 7 ozs. due to Alayna's condition preeclampsia. He stayed in Hillcrest Hospital for a month before he came home from the hospital. I was able to move us in a home in Kent, OH, where I was attending Kent State University.

Alayna later found work, and we lived together for a little over a year. Things didn't work out as planned in our relationship. We decided to coparent, which turned out to be a really great decision for me. We are doing a great job at raising our son. Alayna and I still communicate with one another; we are in good terms.

My 2011–2012 academic achievements allowed me to attend the McNair scholar's research conference in Niagara Falls, New York, in July 2012. Kent State's Trio Student Support Services selected a few students in the program with superior academic achievement to represent KSU in Niagara Falls, New York. It was a wonderful conference that allowed hundreds of students across the country to present their research and to accept awards and certificates. The conference lasted about two or three days and allowed us to view the beautiful Niagara waterfalls and take a ride on the made of the mist boat where the boat took tourist close to the falls, so they can get wet by the mist the falls and water produced.

After returning from the trip, I spent my summer working for the Portage Area Regional Transportation Authority as a service crew worker. Working here made time fly by, and before I knew it, the 2012–2013 school year had arrived. I went to class, and I went to work, going out was cut to a low minimum. I missed a lot of events; I mean a lot of events during senior year due to focusing on school, work, my son, and my home in Kent, Ohio. I had to finish strong. I worked and studied my butt off during fall semester. I had a full class schedule for both fall and spring semester.

My application for graduation was approved. My graduation date was set for May 11, 2013. I purchased my cap and gown and tassel. I took graduation pictures; I attended the spring semester 2013 job and career fall in February 2013. I was set for graduation.

Before I graduated college, I had to do something I've always wanted to do in college that I never had the opportunity to do. Spring break. I went ahead and booked a solo trip to South Beach Miami, Florida, in March 2013. It was a gift to me for all my hard work and accomplishments. I deserved it. I enjoyed the beautiful city, exotic cars, the beautiful beaches, people and night life. My most memorable moment was parasailing over the ocean. It was like paradise. I was miles and miles away from home floating in a parachute like a thing, gliding through the air looking over the beautiful horizon. I didn't have to work or do any schoolwork. I felt free. I even enjoyed being dipped in the ocean on my way down to the boat.

When I returned back to Kent, Ohio, the following week after my Miami trip, I spent a week sharing the details of my trip to family and friends. They were excited to hear about South Beach Miami.

It was the month of April, a month away from my "big day." All my assignments were turned in, and all I had to do was study for final exams next month. I spent the month of April studying for finals and planning my graduation party. The plan was to have a dinner at my mother's house followed by a party bus that would take us to local clubs.

I was invited to attend the Karamu Ya Wahitimu ceremony at the KSU Kiva center April 26, 2013. Karamu Ya Wahitimu is "Swahili for celebration of the graduates. Kelsey Loyva and Trinidy Jeter stated, "The goal of the ceremony was to recognize the AALANA (minority) student's achievement." At Kent State and other national colleges and universities across the board, AALANA graduation rates are lower than other ethnic groups. This is an event to show case and highlight our student's accomplishments.

I was honored to attend the Karamu Ya Wahitimu graduation ceremony.

What made this ceremony unique was that graduates with children were allowed to walk down the aisle and cross the stage with their children. Also as graduates walked across stage to receive their certificate, the announcer read out loud the announcement the graduate had written to be shared with the audience.

Friday April 26, 2013, my son Jaheir (eleven months old at the time) accompanied me at the ceremony along with my two best friends that also attended Kent State. I was the only father AALANA graduate present with his child, every other graduate with their children were women. Jaheir and I stood out, and graduates and ceremony attendees were amazed. We received a lot of attention. People were coming up shaking our hands, telling me congratulations and gave a whole lot of positive comments.

Waiting in line outside the Kiva Auditorium until my name was called to walk down the aisle to the stage. Jaheir and I were greeted by Jacob BYK from the *Daily Kent Stater* (the independent student newspaper of Kent State University) for a photograph. Our picture was featured in the *Daily Kent Stater* on Monday April 29, 2013.

After taking my last final exam as an undergraduate college student on May 09, 2013, I felt an extreme amount of relief. No more homework, studying, group projects, research papers, quizzes, exams, study guides or assignments. I was on my way to becoming a first generation college graduate. Commencement was being held Saturday, May 11, 2013, in the KSU MAC Center at 9:00 a.m.

Saturday morning, I awoke feeling super excited. I took care of my hygiene's, got dressed in my tux shirt, vest, pants, and shoes. Put on my cap and gown and headed out the door for commencement. Accompanying me was my good friend and brother Jayson (a student at KSU). We arrived in the campus and we departed ways once we were inside the MAC center. I went to check in and he went to meet with my family so they all could sit together during the ceremony.

After checking in, I had to find my place in line. College of Arts and Sciences is the largest program at KSU and has thousands of graduates each semester. While finding my spot in line, I was amazed at how many people were graduating that morning. This wasn't like High School at all. I was surrounded by thousands of people that have accomplished the same goal that I have; and that's getting a college degree.

Making our way to the gymnasiums where the ceremony was being held took quite a while. Thousands of students had to be led to their seat. The butterflies started kicking in as I got closer to the gymnasium. This is my moment, the moment I've worked so hard for. As I approached the gym doors, I marched in with music playing in the background, families screaming and yelling (in excitement) for their graduates. I made it to my seat and began looking for my family. In a matter of minutes, I was able to locate them in the top right bleachers, just above where I was standing. I waved at them, and I got teary eyed. I shed a few tears of joy. I knew they were extremely proud of me.

The ceremony lasted about three to four hours long. We had keynote speakers, and we had to wait until each graduate name was called.

It was a long waiting process before lining up to cross the stage. But it was well worth it. When my section/row was called to stand up and exit the gym, to line up outside of the doors leading to the stage, I was really nervous but ready for my moment. While waiting in line outside the doors leading to the stage, I began practicing my victory dance, the dance I would use walking across the stage to receive my degree. Before I knew it, I was up to cross the stage in front of hundreds and hundreds of viewers. The announcer read "Jameel Davis," the spotlight was on. I did my little victory dance across the stage and shook hands with the person giving me my degree. I headed down the long ramp that led to my seat. As I walked back; I waved to my family showing them my degree. I was now a first-generation college graduate. It was one of the most exciting moments of my life. That was one of three ceremonies that was held that day; 4,450 students graduated on May, 11, 2013.

At the conclusion of the ceremony, family and friends joined for hugs and pictures.

I was happy to see and hug my family and friends afterward. I couldn't wait to see, hold, and kiss my mother and son. My grandparents weren't able to make it to the ceremony, but I was anxious to get back home that evening to see them.

We gathered that evening at my mother's house for a wonderful meal she had prepared in celebration of my graduation. Followed dinner, we boarded my party bus and celebrated the rest of the night. "I wore my graduation cap everywhere I went that day and was greeted and congratulated by everyone I came in contact with."

Now that I have graduated from college and earned my degree in Justice Studies, it was time to find a career. I spent the next month (June) applying for jobs and attending interviews. By the end of June, I was frustrated and fed up with applying for jobs and meeting up with job recruiters. Employers said they wanted a candidate with a degree. I got the degree, and now they wanted a candidate with experience. How do I get the experience I need for the positions I'm applying for, if I have been in college for five years obtaining the degree for the position? I gave up and I lost myself. I was stressed and depressed. I had a college degree and could not secure a position. I stayed in the house with my son for a week straight, stressed out about not finding a job. I did not let my one-year-old son see me that way, but everyone else could see I was not myself. I was so stressed that I wrote an article titled, "First Generation College Graduates and the Entry Level Job Market." I wrote this article to tell about the challenges high school graduates and first generation college graduates face upon entering the professional job market.

On July 3, 2013, my friends Jayson Hawkins and Gerrell Jones convinced me to attend our friend Wilson Kuzyk's (Portage County Deputy Sheriff) preindependence day gathering at his parents' home. His parents have a large and beautiful home with a built-in pool and a large outdoor patio. The gathering was held outdoors on the patio and the pool was open to guests. The Kuzyk's neighbors were present at the preindependence day gathering, and their home was just as big as the Kuzyk's. We enjoyed food, drinks, fun, music, and fireworks that were put together by the Kuzyk's family. Amazed by the Kuzyk's home and their neighbors, I was able to meet the Tolbert's (neighbors) after the fireworks presentation. Upon introducing myself, I asked Mr. Tolbert (Principal Consultant, Lucrum INC) what do I have to do in order to live like this? He stated, "Obtain a college degree, secure an entry level position, and work as hard as you can." I knew it was not that simple and that it was more to it. After speaking with him further, I was able to get the answer I was looking for. He said, "Networking." He got to where he is today by networking. It's not about what you know, it's who you know. He told me that I have to reach out to people, so when they come across an open position, they can think of you as the perfect candidate for the position. I then asked how I begin the networking process. He stated, "LinkedIn is a perfect start." Create a profile and connect with me on there. I have never heard of LinkedIn before meeting Mr. Tolbert. LinkedIn is a business-oriented social networking service whose mission is to connect the world's professionals to make them more productive and successful (http://www.linkedin.com/about-us). Mr. Tolbert left me with this. He told me to visit Arlene Schwartz's Personalize Resume Service website at www.aresumes.net to perfect my resume and cover letters and to sharpen up on my interview skills…good luck. I was relieved of stress after the conversation with Mr. Tolbert and was ready to network and apply for jobs again.

I spent the next two days creating a LinkedIn profile, perfecting my resume and cover letters and reviewing the job search information on Arlene Schwartz's Personalize Resume Service website. While browsing her website, I realized why employers either looked past my resume or did not receive them at all. I learned that at most corporations, no live person actually reads resumes. Instead they are scanned into or entered directly into the candidate database by the ATS (Advanced Applicant Tracking Systems). Most systems do nothing with the resumes until they are specifically asked by a recruiter or manager to search through them for a specific job opening. Resumes can sit in the database and never be read by a human being. Only if a recruiter or manager decides to search the database after the hundreds of thousands of resumes are electronically narrowed down to a manageable number (usually less than a hundred), is it possible for someone to actually "read" a candidate's resume. Recruiters who do search databases generally do it only one day per week, and if a candidate's resume didn't come in that day, it will probably be lost in the volume of thousands of resumes that will arrive before the next search day. Resume spamming by applicants has become so common that many recruiters and managers refuse to search the database, since it contains numerous unqualified candidates applying for jobs for which they have no skills. After being burned a few times, many recruiters and managers stick to referrals, niche job boards, and other tools -- they actually abandon searching resumes that come in through the corporate website.

I also learned that applicant tracking systems sort resumes primarily based on the number of keywords in the resume. If candidates fail to use the right keywords there is no chance their resume will be read by a human being (**Arlene Schwartz**, 1997–2013).

On the website, there's a list of words to use and words to not use in your resume and cover letter. In my resume and cover letter, I had used a lot of words from the not to use list. I began extracting the wrong words and replacing them with words to use. While browsing the site, I also found that I was applying for jobs in the least effective way. Arlene Schwartz (1997–2013) stated on her Personalize Resume Service website that responding to job postings on the Internet is a 4–10 percent chance that a candidate will get hired. It was the worst, least effective method to apply for jobs. The best method is networking, finding names of jobs and organizations that are of interest to you in your community, researching names of people in those organizations who have the power to hire you, developing a plan to best approach that person, send a hard copy of your resume, and cover letter and follow up with a phone call. Network by telephone, in person, by e-mail, and on business networking sites like LinkedIn.com but focus more on telephone and in person contacts. I also learned to send handwritten thank-you notes within twenty-four hours after an interview.

After obtaining my degree, applying to job postings on the internet was my only method for applying to companies. Upon reviewing the job search information on Arlene Schwartz's Personalize Resume Service website, I began applying for jobs the most effective way. I used the Internet to research some local companies and the names of people in those organizations that have the power to hire. I sent them hard copies of my resume and cover letters and followed up with a phone call. I also connected with them on LinkedIn. Some of the companies and individuals in whom I have contacted were Administrative Officer Eric Tranter, at the Federal Bureau of Investigations Cleveland Division for the Operational Support Technician position; Robin McKnight, Recruiter at Caesars Entertainment Corporation for a Security position and the Ohio Department of Youth Services for the Youth Specialist position.

In a short amount of time, I received feedback from all the companies I mentioned earlier. My good friend Latrice Lett (Employee of the FBI Cleveland Division) notified me that the FBI Cleveland Division is on a hiring freeze until the summer of 2014, but Mr. Eric Tranter is highly interested in meeting with me once the hiring freeze is over. The Ohio Department of Youth Services notified me that I was qualified for the Youth Specialist position and that I had to travel to Orient, Ohio, to take a written exam. I had planned on attending, but something came up and I was unable to make the drive to Orient, Ohio. Robin McKnight contacted me for a phone interview and at the conclusion of the phone interview; I was scheduled for a panel interview at the Horseshoe Casino here in Downtown Cleveland, Ohio on July 16, 2013. Prior to my interview, Robin McKnight notified me that Horseshoe was looking for upbeat and positive candidates for the positions.

My panel interview was conducted by three human resources representatives.

It was not an ordinary panel interview, where the candidate was on one side of a table and three interviewers were on the other. Also, it was not a question and answer interview. The interview was conducted in a large room and present were over fifty-plus candidates for different hiring positions in the Horseshoe Casino. They were also present for their panel interview. Everyone was dressed in formal attire with their portfolios. We were not expecting for our panel interview to be conducted like this. Three human resources representatives came and sat behind a small table and faced the candidates in the room. Each human resources representative introduced themselves and explained how the panel interview will be conducted. They said they will each pick three topics off a sheet they had in front of them (one each), and we all have to do what they selected. The first human resources representatives stated that we had to meet someone new in the room and introduce them to everyone in the room. We had to sell them.

I met a young lady by the name of Deianna Brown. She was a graduate of the Cleveland School of Arts, and she had just returned from New York. She was in New York pursuing her music career; she loves to sing. After getting some background on her, I began telling her about me: name, age, education, children, goals, hobbies, etc. After our introduction, we got involved in a conversation where I was offering her motivation and inspiration support. One of my strengths. I love to help others by giving words of wisdom and encouragement. Our conversation was interrupted by one of the human resources representatives; they were ready to begin the panel interview. My partner and I decided to go first. I decided to introduce her first. I wanted to be noticed from the start of the interview to the end. With my public speaking skills I have developed in college, I was comfortable and ready. I delivered the introduction of Deianna Brown with enthusiasm and with confidence as if I had known her already. I sold her the best way I knew how. It was her turn to introduce me. Right off the back she told them to hire me. She stated, "You should hire him right now, he's perfect for whatever job he's applying for." She then said Jameel is very outgoing and intelligent, etc. Listening to him speak, he should become a public speaker. She told them my age and that I was a recent first generation college graduate of Kent State University. She sold me like a new car at a car show. I was not expecting that at all. Her introduction of me got me in the human resources rep's spotlight. No other candidate was introduced like I was introduced.

The second human resource representative stated that we had to act out an animal until someone in the audience guessed it correctly. No one was expecting this at all. Once again, I decided to go first. I love to act silly in front of people and besides, I'm upbeat and positive. I acted out a coyote. It was fun watching others in their formal attire making a fool of themselves in front of strangers. The last representative stated that we had to sing out loud our favorite line of a favorite song. I did not volunteer to go first this time because I had a brain fart; a song I knew did not come to mind until after ten people had went. I ended up singing a line in the song "Color of Love" by Boyz II Men. "Like a bridge over troubled, troubled water…you stood beside me and your love did not falter and then the angel, the angel in you gave the strength to know that I will get through." At the conclusion of the last singer, the human resources representative exited the room to make their decision. When they arrived back in the room, they called names of individuals and told them to leave the room. The ones, who left, were not returning. Every one remaining, were new employees of the Horseshoe Casino. Everyone was excited. Our start date was set for August 26, 2013, and we would be at-will employees, which means that we will not be under a contract and will not have any benefits. That also mean we could be asked to leave at any time without notice.

July 17, 2013, Jeff Rotsky (Founder of the Rotsky Foundation for Mentors) and Joe Klir (Jeff's Assistant) contacted me and asked if I could speak at the Rotsky Foundation's Sixteenth Annual Silent Auction and Dinner on July 19, 2013. They wanted me to share my success story. Out of hundreds and hundreds of individuals that went through the program, I was selected as the keynote speaker by the founder and his partner to speak on behalf of the Rotsky Foundation for Mentors. I was amazed. With such short notice, I was not able to prepare a speech. However, I knew once I opened my mouth, the right words would flow right out and everyone would be tuned in. I also knew that if I told a great story, people would spend big on the merchandise and trips being auctioned off and that the Rotsky Foundation for Mentors would be able to help more people succeed like myself.

On the day of the silent auction and dinner, I was amazed by the number of people present. It was a big turnout. I was seated and then I helped myself to some food and refreshments. After everyone was just about finished eating, Jeff Rotsky took the floor and welcomed everyone to the sixteenth annual silent auction and dinner. He then went on and explained the details about the event. At the conclusion of his introduction and speech about the auction, he introduced me to the audience as the keynote speaker for the evening. He spoke to the audience about when we first met, gave them a little background about me and then told them how I matured into a successful individual. It was heartwarming listening to a millionaire, the founder of the Rotsky Foundation for Mentors, tell a wonderful story about me to a large diverse audience. I never knew anyone who knew me so well. I had a great feeling inside, I felt very important. Everyone gave me a round of applause as Jeff welcomed me to the front of the room.

I began by thanking Jeff for the awesome introduction and I got right into my success story.

I spoke about the challenges I faced growing up in the city of Cleveland, Ohio, the challenges I faced in school, and how I fought through them; my transition from high school to college and the obstacles I faced and how I overcame them. I also explained how the Rotsky Foundation for Mentors was my motivation to succeed and how it is the foundation of my success.

At the end of my speech, I received a standing ovation from the audience. Everyone was smiling and applauding and very proud of what I have achieved. I then told the audience that I was looking for a career opportunity and that it would be greatly appreciated if someone gave me some good resources and tips. As I walked back to my seat, people were telling me "Great Job," "Great Speech," "Keep up the Good Work," etc.

My good friend David Kowolski's mentor Jack O'Breza, one of the Board of Directors for the Rotsky Foundation for Mentors, was present at the silent auction and dinner; and I had the pleasure of speaking to him about securing a career position. During our conversation, I raised a question, "How do I get the experience I need for the job I want if I have been in college for five years trying to obtain a degree for that position?" I do not remember his direct response to the question. But I do remember him telling me that the next time I have an interview, to sell myself and sell me good. Something I have not been doing at interviews. He told me that employers and recruiters get bored during interviews because candidates give the same boring responses when they are asked to tell about themselves and how they can benefit the company. Most say that they are hardworking, dependable, organized, etc. He said employers hear that all the time. They want someone that is different from the majority. Someone who could sell themself, the company and who could make them say, he is the one for the position.

I then told Jack that I need help selling myself during interviews and he was willing to help. He spent about fifteen minutes helping me prepare for my next interview. I remember him telling me to approach the interview with energy and to speak with enthusiasm as if I had known them prior to the interview. Within the short time frame, he was able to help me prepare a little speech to give at my next interview, when asked to tell about you and how can I benefit the company. I was grateful that I was able to receive valuable interview tips from a sports journalist. Upon my conversation with Jack O'Breza, another familiar face, an ex-police officer met with me. She suggested that I get on the Cuyahoga County website and apply to all the open positions. I thanked her for the information.

The first of August had rolled around, and while waiting on the twenty-sixth day to come around so I can began work at the Horseshoe Casino, I visited the Cuyahoga County website and applied to the Corrections Officer position that was posted by the Cuyahoga County Sheriff's Department. The job came with full government benefits and a good starting salary. Two days later before I had the chance to send off a hard copy of my resume and cover letter, I received a call from the Cuyahoga County Human Resources Department stating that I was invited to take the civil service exam for the Corrections Officer position the following day.

I arrived at the Justice Center to take my exam. Upon my arrival, I met with a guy by the name of Michael Brown (human resources analysis) at the Cuyahoga County human resources department along with eight other Individuals. I was the youngest. He escorted us through the corrections center and to the classroom where we would be taking our exam. He then explained to us that our exam will be taken on a computer covering reading, mathematics, and grammar. He stated each section is timed and that we had to score a seventy-five or better on the exam. He also said that whoever passed the exam would receive a phone call from him within the next business day and move forward with the hiring process. If you did not pass, you had to wait six months to reapply.

I was nervous at the time of the exam because I did not know what to expect, and I did not have time to prepare. At the start of exam, I began to feel comfortable about the outcome for the exam because the exam contained material that was taught in the ninth grade. I finished each section in the time frame given and after the last person finished his exam, the human resources guy escorted us back to the main lobby of the justice center and told us that he will be in contact with those whom have passed the exam.

Five minutes after leaving the Justice Center, while in route to home, I received a phone call from the human resources guy stating that I had passed the exam and that he wanted to schedule a panel interview that consisted of him, the jail sergeant and one of the associate jail wardens. He also notified me of the steps in the hiring process: panel interview, jail tour, two weeks of training, both classroom and field. My panel interview was scheduled for the following Monday.

On Monday August 05, 2013, I met with Associate Warden McAuthor, Jail Sergeant Price, and Human Resources Analysis Michael Brown guy in a conference room. With the interview tips I received from Arlene Schwartz Personalized Resume Service website and the interview tips I received from Jack O'Breza, I knew was I was walking out of there with a job as a corrections officer. Hopping right into the interview, I was upbeat and positive. My eye contact was on point; I had a good choice of words and tone of voice when answering questions from the panel. I was calm, relaxed and smiling. I even made them laugh. Most of all, I sold myself like I was an item at an auction event. They answered all of the questions I had prepared for them. They were amazed by the intelligent upbeat, young man they had before them. After the interview, I was asked to wait in the waiting area until they made their final decision regarding me securing the position. Moments later, the human resources guy notified me of their decision and offered me the position of a corrections officer at the Cuyahoga County Sheriff's Department. I was excited and anxious to begin work. Before the offer was official, I had to complete a jail tour in which I completed the following day. After my jail tour, I contacted Robin McKnight the Recruiter at the Horseshoe Casino and the Caesars recruitment team and said:

> Hello, my name is Jameel Davis. I would like to thank the recruiting team and the interviewing panel for selecting me to become part of the world's largest and most prestigious gaming company; Caesars Entertainment Inc.
>
> Unfortunately, I will not be working for Horseshoe Cleveland. I understood when signing my offer letter that I would be an at-will employee with no contract of employment or guarantee of continued employment at any time. Horseshoe Cleveland is one of many companies I have applied to after receiving my college degree in early May 2013. During the Horseshoe hiring process, my skills and qualifications qualified me for a full-time government position. For job security purposes, I went ahead and signed a contract of employment for the agency.
>
> Horseshoe Cleveland's recruitment team, is one of the best recruitment teams I have witnessed. I will encourage others whom are upbeat and positive to apply to such a wonderful company. I enjoyed my interview with the interview panel and

all the other candidates for employment on July 16, 2013.

Once again I would like to thank you for considering me for employment with your organization. Good luck on the company's success and may the company continue to achieve top and bottom line results.

Respectfully Yours,
Jameel Davis

August 24, 2013, my mother gave birth to Jason Daniels Jr. My sister, and I now had a baby brother. Our mother was used to having kids in the home and since my sister and I are adults, and are no longer living in the home, she was lonely, even though she had a partner. She was thirty-seven years young and wanted another child.

I was notified within two weeks of my start date for the Corrections officer position. My start date was set for September 03, 2013. At the start of training, the eight individuals I took the civil service exam with, were not present. Either they failed the exam or they passed and had a poor background check. I completed my drug test and my two weeks of training and was now a corrections officer for the Cuyahoga county sheriff's department. My college, community, extracurricular activities, service, employment, including my leadership, citizenship, honors and awards have helped contribute toward my career goal by preparing me to be professional, hardworking, reliable, dedicated and committed to the offered position. I posted my new position on LinkedIn, and Mr. Tolbert (Kuzyk's Neighbor) sent me a message on LinkedIn that said:

> *Hi, Jameel, I saw you're now Corrections Officer II at Cuyahoga County Sheriff's Department and wanted to say congratulations. Best of luck!*

Upon my first day of work in the Cuyahoga Corrections Center, I knew I would be supervising inmates that came from the same background as I did. Besides supervising inmates within the Correction Center in all daily activities, my personal goal as a corrections officer prior to starting was to inspire and help pretrial felons and sentenced misdemeants mature into successful, responsible adults.

I have been employed as a corrections officer for over a year now.

Over the past year, I have been providing inspirational, spiritual, emotional, and family support to the inmates that I have been supervising. I provided many with tips on finding jobs and housing. I have used my crisis intervention skills to help inmates who were suffering from depression, anxiety and whom were suicidal. I am honored to have helped my first suicide victim at the Cuyahoga County Corrections Center change his thoughts about killing himself. I knew that if I could help him, I could help many other individuals in crisis. I have developed a positive relationship with many inmates in the corrections center: some who have went to prison and some who have went home. I have earned my respect from many inmates of all ages and races in the Cuyahoga County Corrections officer at such a young age.

The inmates that I have helped here at the Cuyahoga County Corrections Center have inspired me to write my success story. I wanted to produce a project of my own that could inspire youth and individuals that live in similar environments, and that attend similar schools as I did growing up, mature into successful, and responsible adults. It's called the Cuyahoga County Corrections Center and I'm willing to help as many individuals as I can correct their lifestyles. The Cuyahoga County Corrections Center is just a starting point; I have bigger plans for my community.

As a young educated African American man growing up in Cleveland, Ohio, I feel that it is important to help young men and women in various communities grow to become successful educated individuals. Many people have helped pave my way to success and it is only right to pass information that was given to me to those who are in need.

One evening in December 2013, while spending some quality time with my mother at home, she and I decided to look up my father on the social networking site Facebook. After searching "John Chavers," we observed that he had about three accounts. We then decided to view each profile to see which one he was most active on. The first two accounts had no activity. He was active on the third account. I then navigated down his page and seen a post written to Aziah Chavers. The post said, "Aziah, this is your Dad ..." I immediately showed my mother. I then clicked on Aziah's profile and her picture popped up on the screen. I then told my mother that she looks very familiar. So I decided to search Aziah on my Twitter and Instagram. I then found that we were following each other on both Twitter and Instagram. I sent her a message on both accounts that said, "Hey, Aziah, can you give me a call, it's important. I think I'm your brother." An hour or so later, I received a phone call from her, and we spoke about us being siblings and confirmed our dad's information (name, birthday, descriptive features, etc.). She then told me, she was currently in Nashville, Tennessee, attending Tennessee State University studying Biology and that she would be in Cleveland the next day for winter break. Before her arrival in Cleveland the next day, I received a call from Aziah's mother (Mrs. Teresa Matthews) whom is currently living in the Cleveland area and suggested that we (Aziah, she, and I) meet that evening before I went in for work. I told Mrs. Matthews that I worked at the Justice Center as a corrections officer and she said she worked in the Justice Center as well but in the prosecutor's office as a victims advocate. She said that she gets off at 5:00 p.m. and that we could meet in her office. I didn't have to clock in until five forty-five that evening. We all met in her office that evening before work. I had met my sister for the first time. It was a very emotional feeling because my sister that was raised with me, and I have a very strong bond and I've missed out on so much with my sister Aziah. When we sat in the office of Aziah's mother, we began talking about our father who wasn't much to talk about because he wasn't in her life either, then gave some background information. I gave Aziah and her mom a brief biography about me and spoke on my recent accomplishments. Aziah then picked up a notified me that she will be graduating from Tennessee State University May 10, 2014. "Even though we've never met, she's following her big brother's footsteps." I told her I would be present at her graduation (I did attend). I was not able to stay long, become I needed to be at work. I was invited over for Christmas for a meal and to meet the rest of her family. The next day or so, I took Aziah out to Dave and Busters for food, fun and games. We spent the time making up for lost time and getting to know one another better. The next time we met up was on Christmas Eve when my son Jaheir and I were invited over to meet Aziah's family. After the greetings and introductions, we sat down enjoyed a small meal along with a glass of wine. We shared stories and a little laughter. Christmas afternoon, I was back over, and I arrived with gifts and money for my sister. I also gave a card with money to Aziah's family, not that they needed it, but it's the thought that counts. I had to cut the visit short because I had to report to work. The meeting of Aziah and her family was a Christmas miracle. Aziah headed back to Nashville on December 27, 2013, to report back to her place of employment. Since Christmas, Aziah and I have kept in contact via phones calls, texts, and social media. Both of my sisters have added each other on the social network Instagram and have kept in contact.

Early April 2014, I picked up the book *Rich Dad Poor Dad* that was given to me by my mentor Leon Anderson III (President of Sports and Spine Physical Therapy) back when I was in the ninth grade. I attempted to read the book then but couldn't because it was boring, which caused me to lose focus, and I didn't understand what I was reading. Reading it as a young adult, I completely understand the meaning of the book. After graduating college, I concluded that my learning was over and that I can work and save for the rest of my life and to prepare for retirement. *Rich Dad Poor Dad* taught me there's another subject in life I needed to learn, and it's not taught in schools. Financial Literacy. How to have money work for you instead of you working for money and making your boss richer. *Rich Dad Poor Dad* taught me the difference between assets and liabilities. Assets put money in your pocket; liabilities take money out of your pocket. The rich acquire assets, and the poor and middle class acquire liabilities that they think are assets. Reading *Rich Dad Poor Dad* has taught me to lower my expenses and to cut my spending so that I could invest my money into money-generating assets. From the book, I've also learned to reward (buy luxuries) myself later after my asset column is equal to or greater than my monthly expenses. *Rich Dad Poor Dad* led me to read *Real Estate Riches* by Dolf de Roos, and *Creating Wealth* by Robert. G. Allen. All three books have taught me more about financial literacy than any other educational program I have attended combined. They have taught me how to invest in real estate, stocks, bonds, money market certificates, rare coins, and a few other money generating assets. I've learned how to find real estate properties, negotiate prices with the seller, buy properties using zero to little money down, find good tenants, depreciate properties on your taxes, manage properties, refinance properties, sell properties, develop corporations (asset protection house), create living trusts, create IRA accounts, children partnerships, limited partnerships, invest in rare coins, and much more.

There was me thinking that all my learning was complete after five years of college and me thinking working and saving will give me the American Dream (Financial Independence). Then it came to reality that saving money wouldn't create wealth and that I was stuck in the rat race. As mentioned in *Rich Dad Poor Dad*.

Robert G. Allen's Principals of Education which guide readers in search for knowledge states, "If you think education is expensive, try ignorance." In this principal, he said, "Some education is too expensive." In his opinion, most of what is taught at universities is enormously expensive not only in money but in time. And the kind of education that takes a long time to make you ill prepared to deal with the harsh realities of life is almost worse than ignorance. In his opinion, he also believed the seminar approach to adult education is much more efficient. Although seminars take much less time, they can be expensive. When you add up the tuition, travel, and hotel expenses, it is not difficult to drop $1,000. But the best seminars teach more in two days about real nitty-gritty of building wealth than most people learn in a decade of university training. After graduating from College and looking at the big picture, I agree with Robert G. Allen's opinions 100 percent. Many people do have a hard time paying even small amounts of money for knowledge—especially those that are sealed in college. Robert G. Allen said it best, "So many will step over dollars to pick up pennies."

Three books taught me how to get out the rat race; five years of college only taught me how to race along other rats. College has also taught me about perseverance—enough to know that if I could make it through five years of college, I could do anything. I can't fault the general knowledge I gained in college, like Robert G. Allen mentioned in his book *Creating Wealth*, it have helped me mature over the years. *Rich Dad Poor Dad, Real Estate Riches,* and *Creating Wealth* gave me motivation to action. I'm now investing my time and money on other investment books and seminars, so I can learn as much as I can about financial literacy before being released from the lab full of rats and on my journey to financial independence.

1. The man who does not work for the love of work but only for money is not likely to make money nor to find much fun in life. —Charles M. Schwab
2. Don't compete. Create. Find out what everyone else is doing and then don't do it. —Joel Weldon
3. Come to the edge, He said.
   They said, we are afraid.
   Come to the edge, He said.
   They Came.
   He pushed them...and they flew. —Guillaume Apollinaire

What I want my readers to take from this success story is to never give up, no matter how hard it gets. Always ask questions and ask for help. Be open to learn for the rest of your life; don't lock your brain from learning after your graduate from whatever educational program you attend. There are many resources available to help you achieve your goals and to help you become a better individual. I got to where I am today by never giving up, by asking for help and asking questions. Let my story help you be the change in society. Strive for success and be great.

WORK CITED

Allen, Robert, G. (1983). *Creating wealth*. New York, NY: Simon and Schuster.

Cuyahoga County Metropolitan Housing Authority. (2014). *What we do*. Retrieved online on May 14, 2014, from https://www.cmha.net/aboutus/index.aspx

Hoffman, R. (May 05, 2003). *LinkedIn*. Retrieved online May 16, 2014, from https://www.linkedin.com/about-us

Kiyosaki, Robert, T., and Lechter, S, L. (1997, 1998). *Rich dad poor dad*. New York, NY: Warner Books, CASHFLOW Technologies Inc.

Roos, D, De. (2001). *Real Estate Riches*: How to become rich using your banker's money (Rich Dad's Advisors)

Schwartz, Arlene (1997–2013). *Personalized resume service*. Retrieved online on March 29, 2014, from http://www.aresumes.net/best-methods/areyourresumesread.html

ABOUT THE AUTHOR

Jameel Davis was born to Louise Davis, whom was only 13 years old at the time. He grew up in the densely populated urban communities that were plagued by high violence and high poverty in Cleveland, Ohio. Even though he was surrounded by negative influences that gave him little hope for success, Jameel managed to avoid incarceration and excel in the poor educational programs provided by the Cleveland Municipal School District. From there, he went on an excelled in a Higher Learning Program that most individuals in poverty dominated environments fail to attend.

Jameel became self-disciplined, got rid of the negative influences that were surrounding him and became a successful, educated individual. Jameel says, "Looking back over the years of my life, I have experienced many phases of failure and success. Those experiences have helped me become a wonderful individual, father, motivational speaker, role model, mentor, businessman, family man, a leader and now an Author."

CPSIA information can be obtained
at www.ICGtesting.com
Printed in the USA
BVHW031253240919
559270BV00001B/21/P